I0751984

"What Do You Do With A Donkey?"

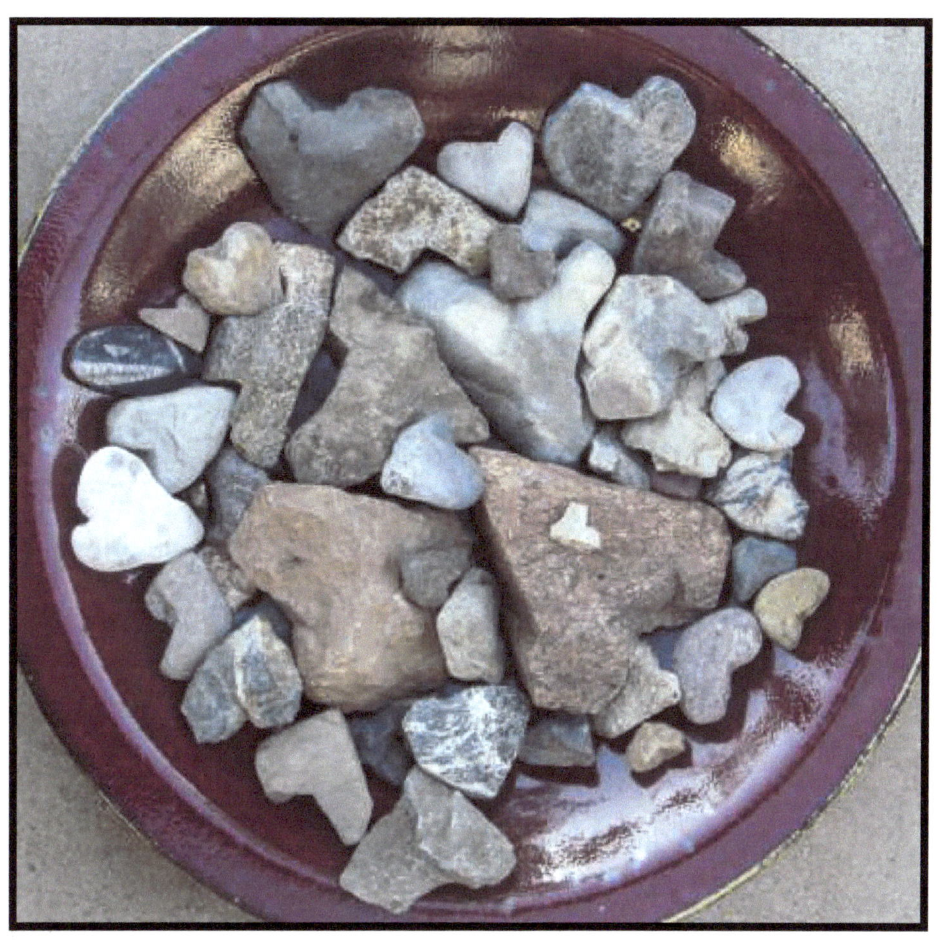

'Have a Heart Publishing'
Wildomar, CA 92595

Visit my website at www.JaniceCarabinePhotography.com

16 15 14 13 4 3 2 1 First Edition

Editor: David Carabine, Peyton Monsen
Book Designer: Janice Carabine
Image Credits: Janice Carabine

Library of Congress - 2013914324
US & Publisher Liaison Division
Cataloging in Publication Program
101 Independence Avenue, S.E.
Washington, DC 20540-4283

ISBN: 978-0-615-86018-3

Dedicated to:

Christopher Thomas Carabine

I miss you and love you always.

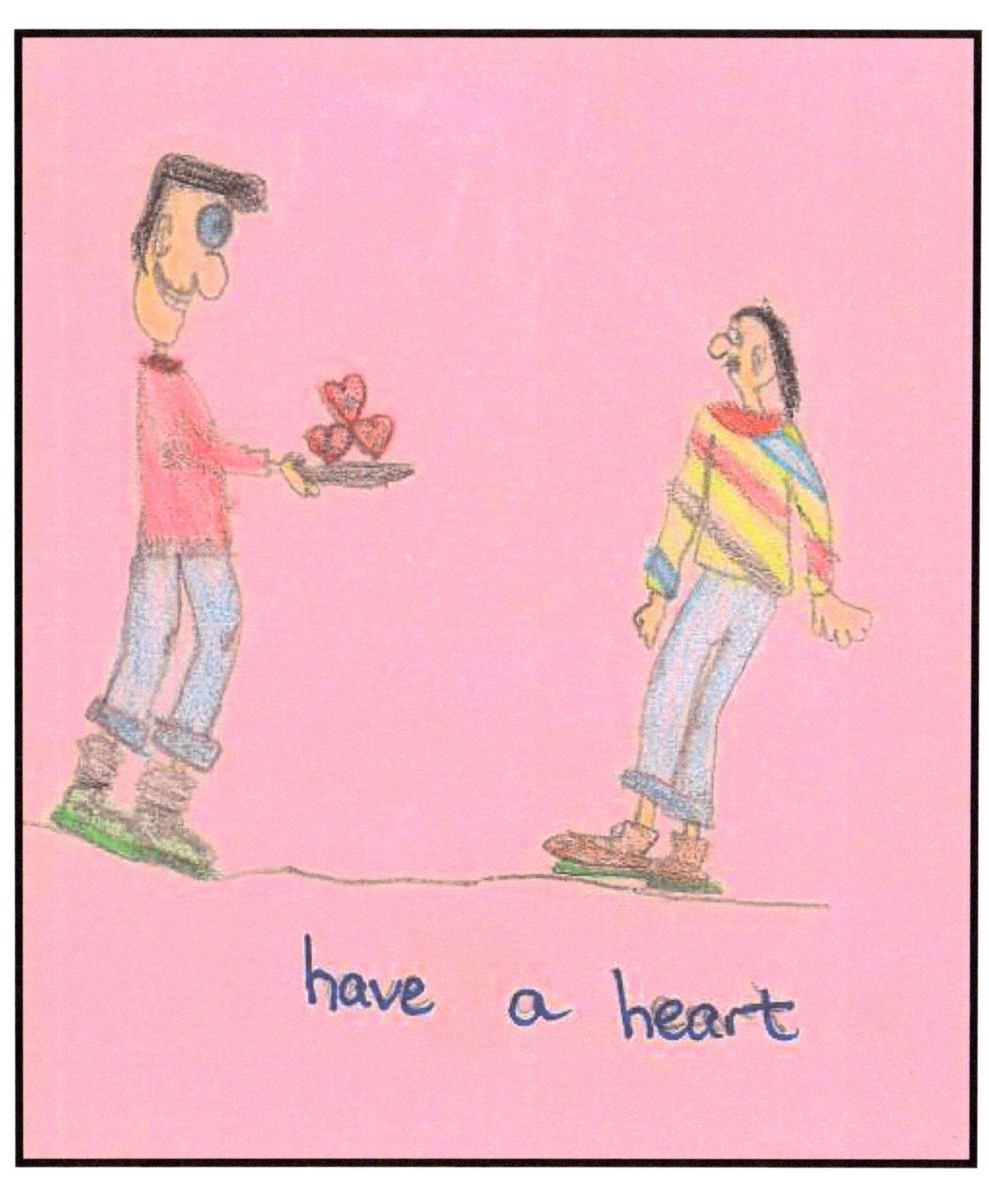

What Do You Do With A Donkey?"

Peyton and her brother, Hunter, went to visit their grandparent's ranch in California. They have four donkeys at the ranch. Great Gramma, Mary, walked with Peyton to go see the donkeys in their pens.

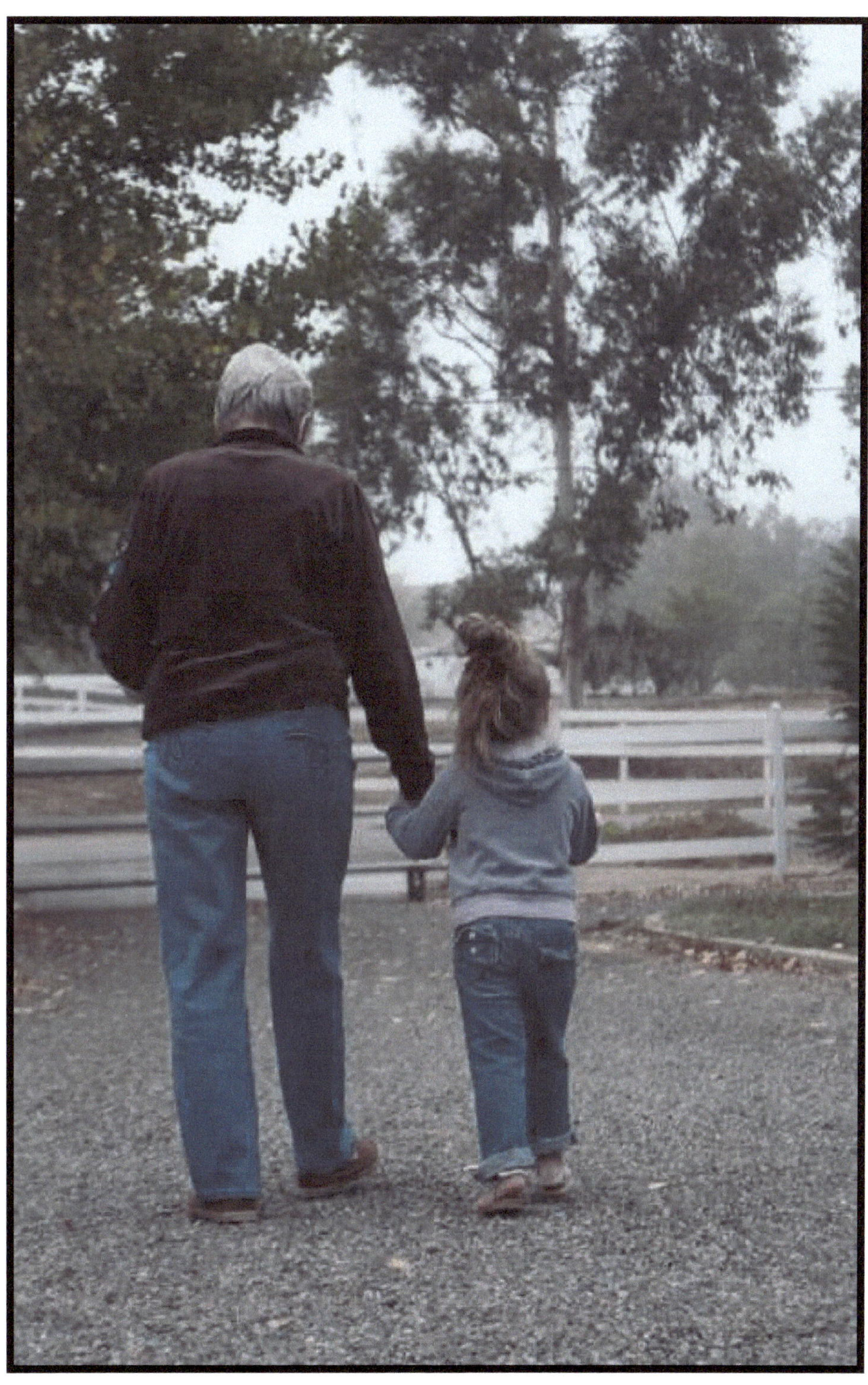

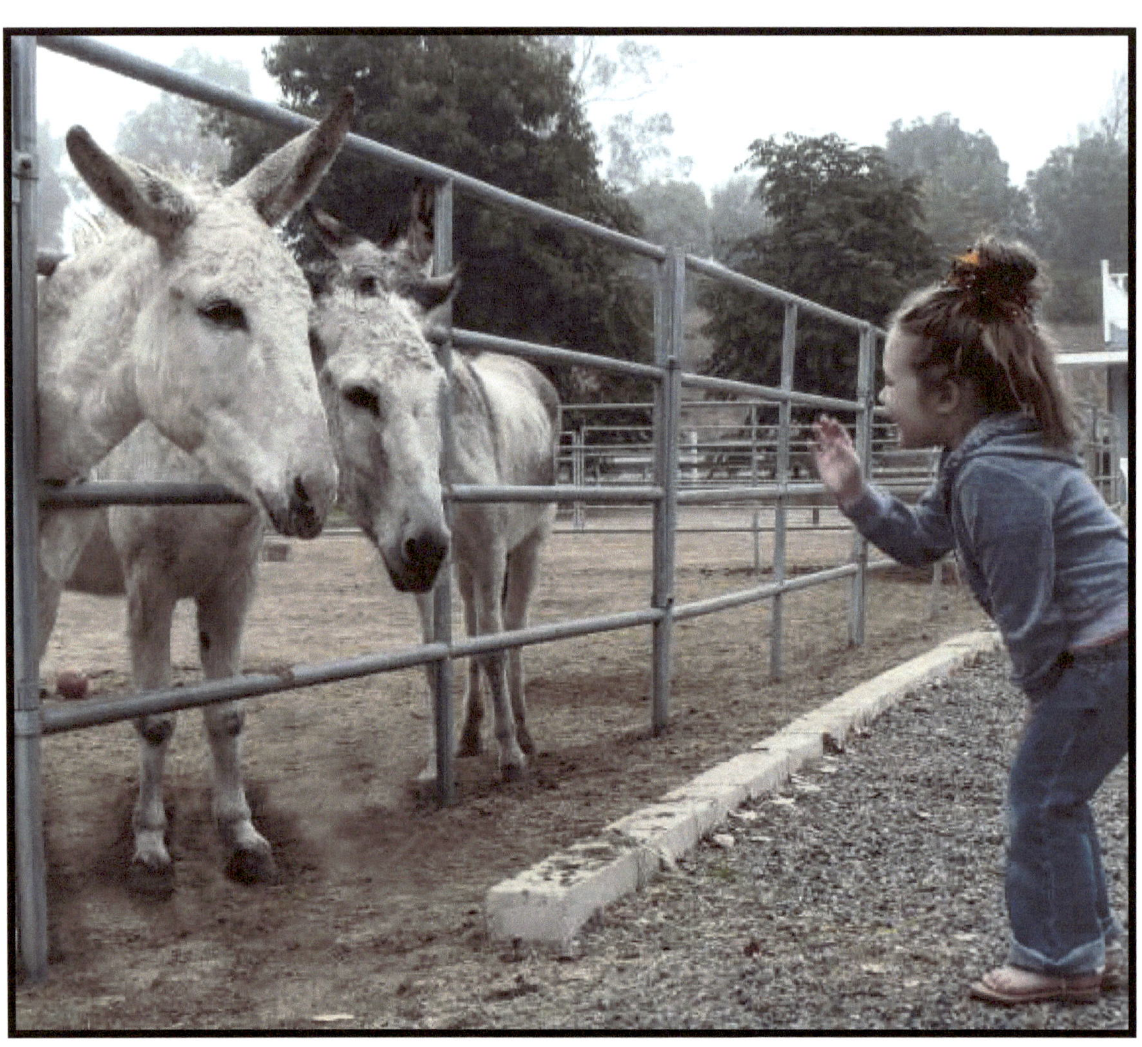

"HELLOOOO DONKEYS,

What are you doing?"

Peyton shouted loudly.

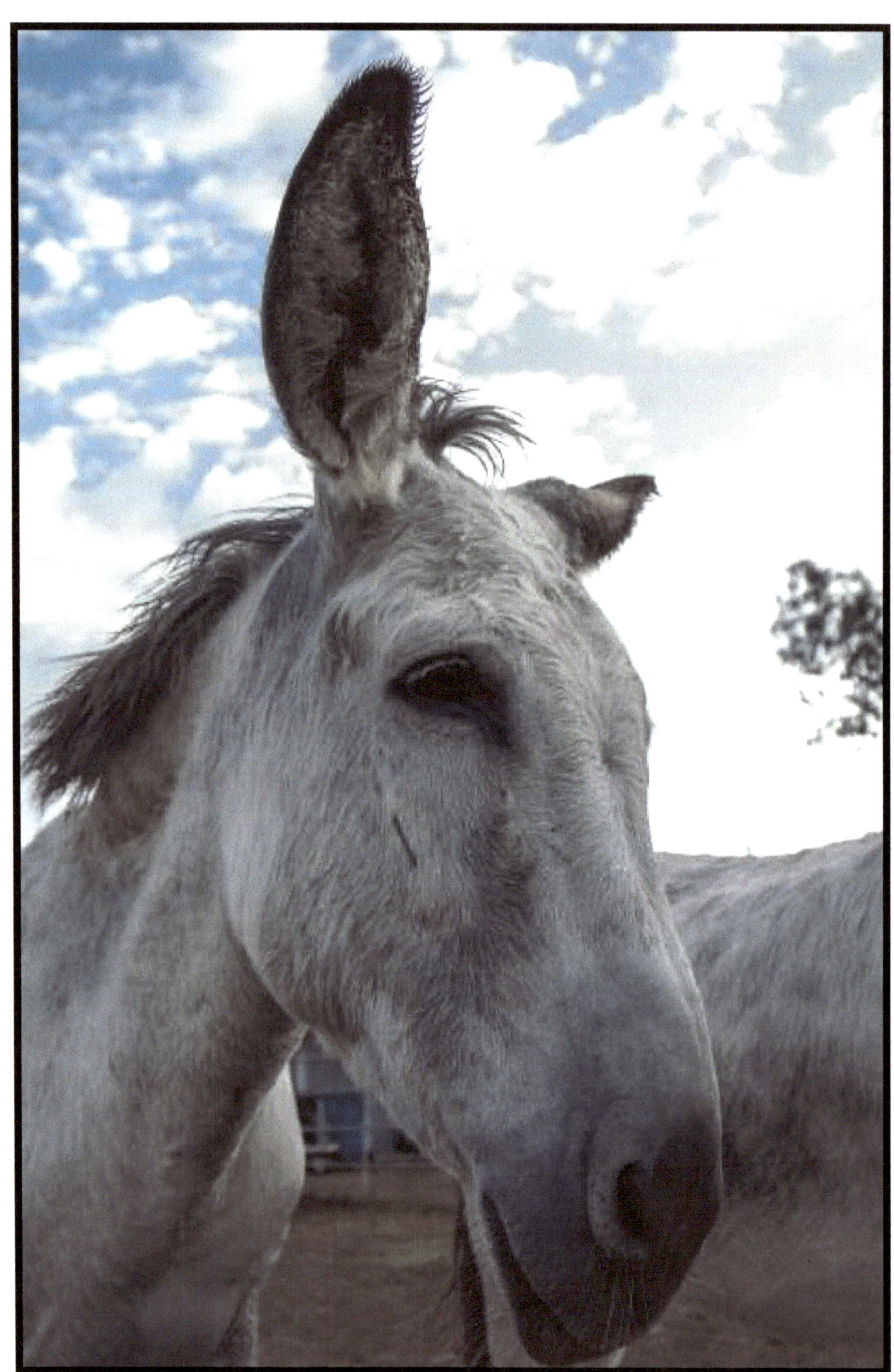

While watching the donkeys, Peyton noticed something very unusual about them.

"Donkeys have really tall ears don't they Great Gramma? They reach way up into the sky."

Great Gramma said, "Yes Peyton, their ears are very tall and the donkeys like it when you rub them."

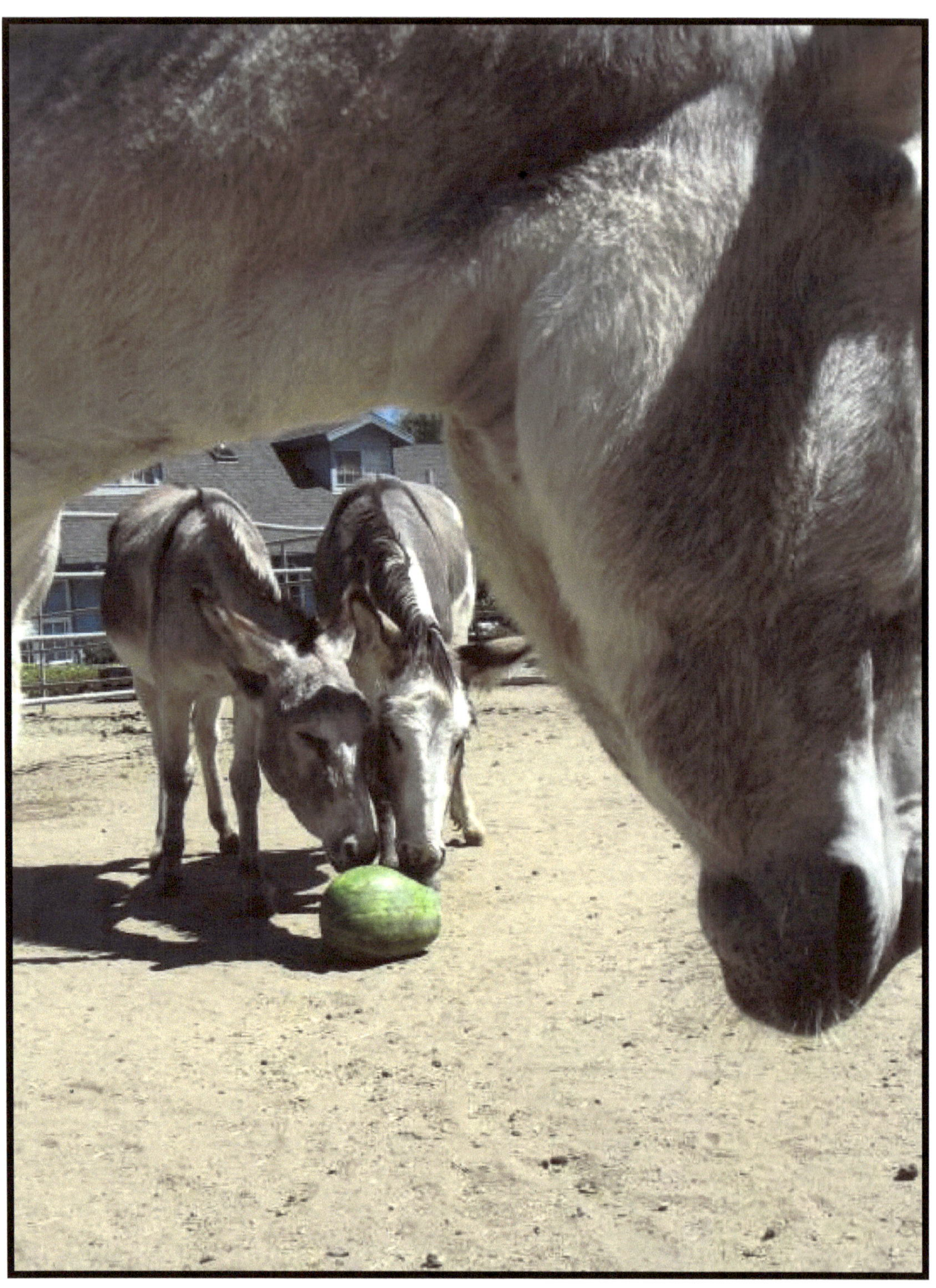

"Do they like carrots?" Peyton asked Great Gramma.

"Yes, they love carrots and apples, ginger snaps, strawberries, watermelon, licorice, candy canes, peanuts, bananas, oranges and even donuts."

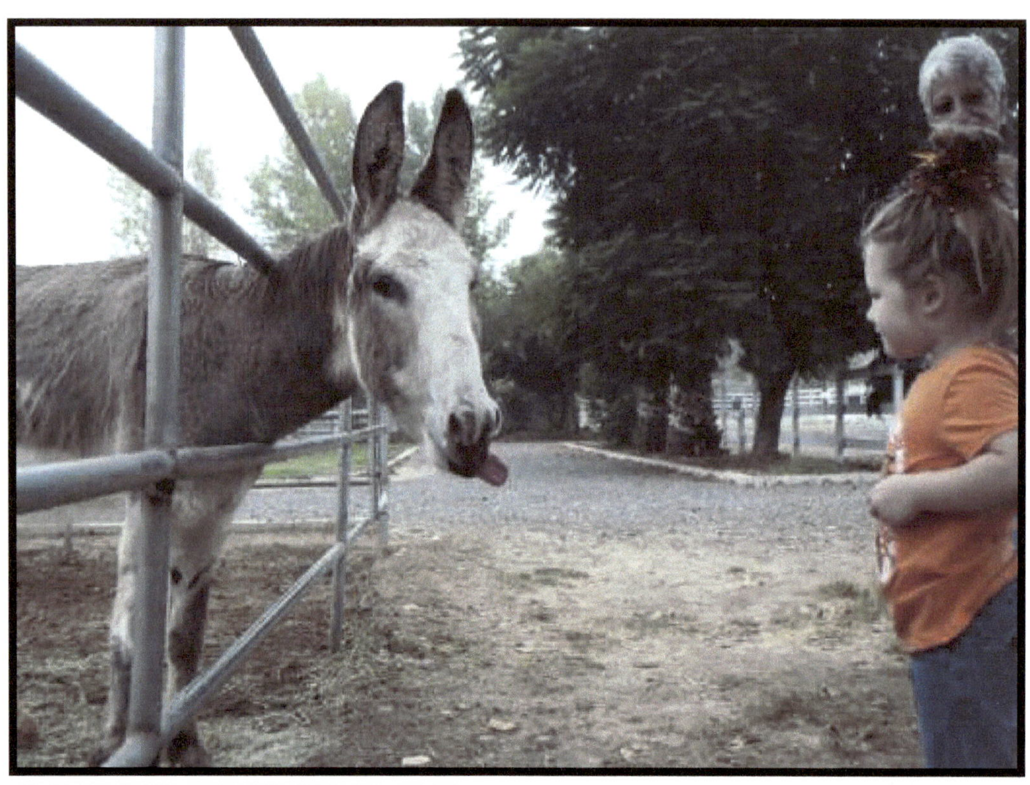

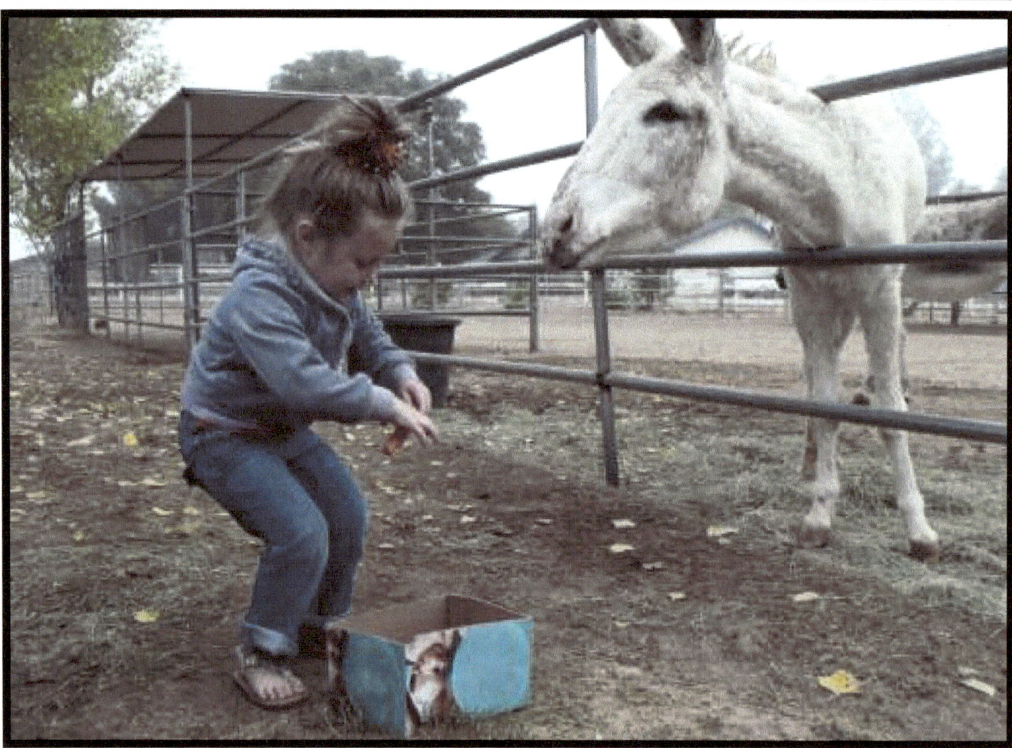

Peyton had brought some carrots and oranges with her and she threw the carrots into their pen. Peyton and Great Gramma laughed as they watched them eat all the carrots.

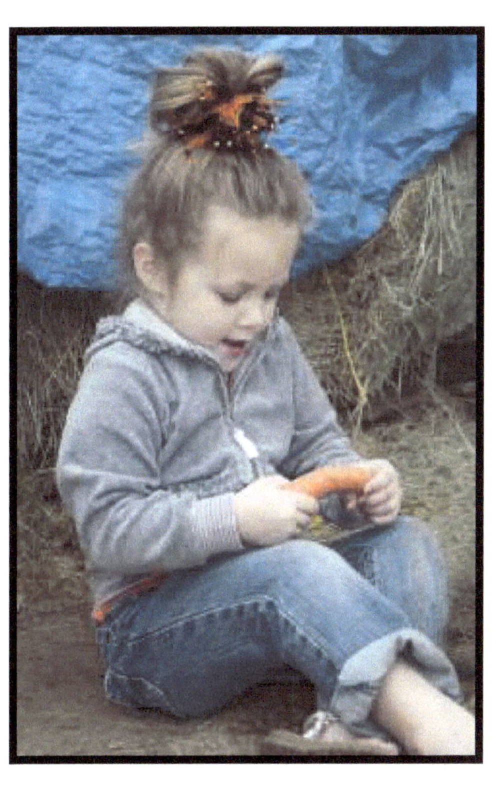

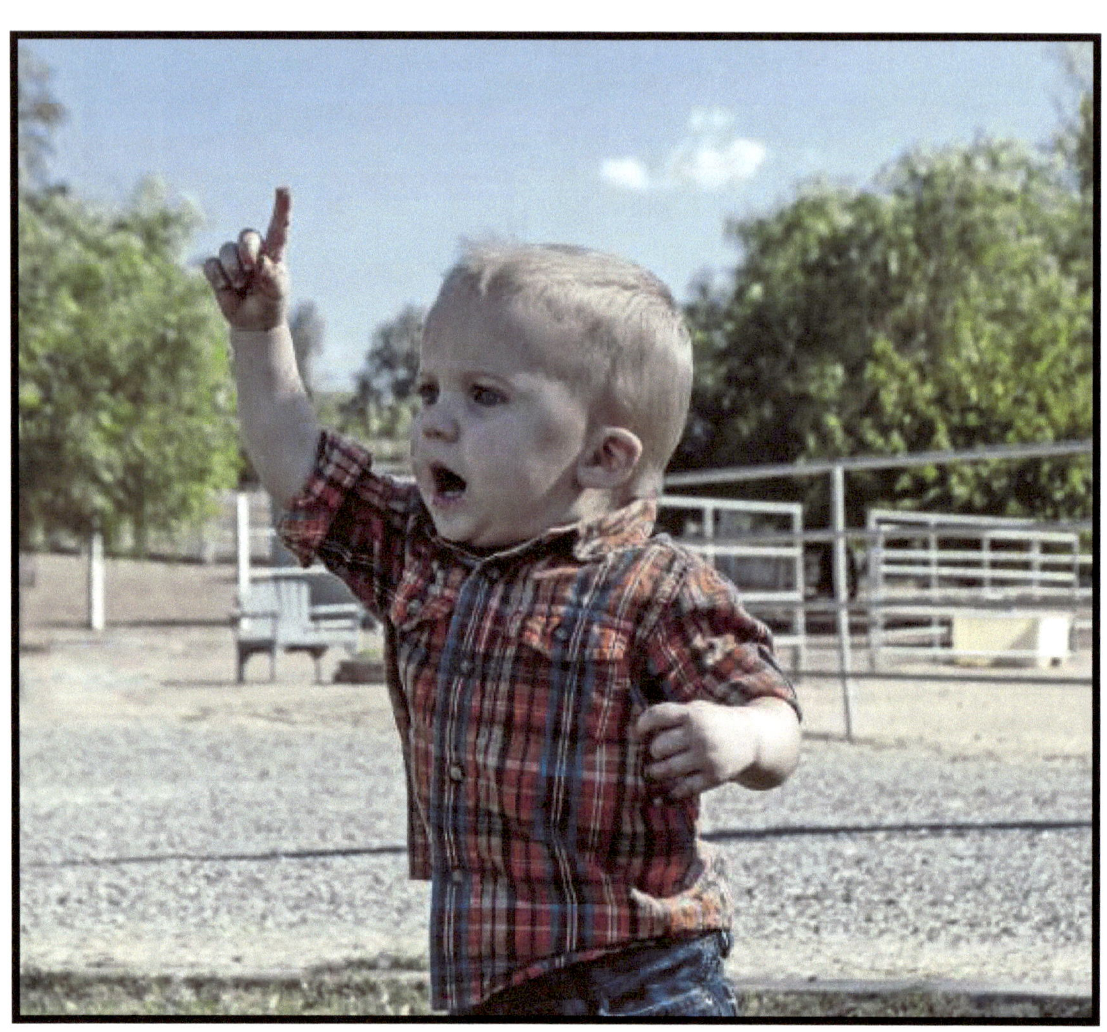

Hunter, Peyton's little brother, came running across the yard to see what Peyton was doing with Great Gramma.

"Wait for me - I want to feed the donkeys too!", he said.

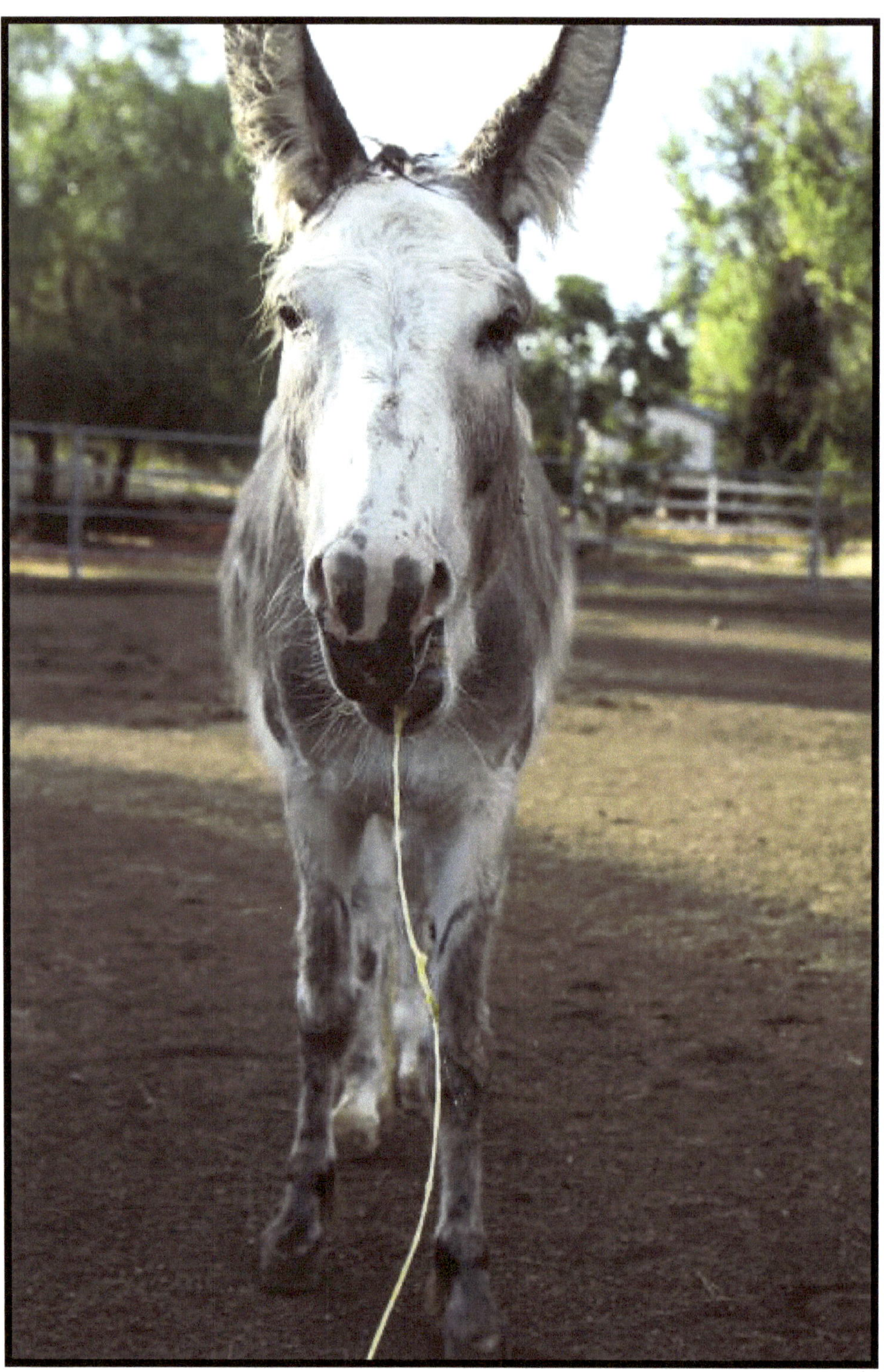

Together, they fed the girl donkeys more carrots. Then Andy came over to see what was going on. He ate an orange that Gramma had in her pocket. The orange juice dripped and dripped out of his mouth and made them all laugh so hard.

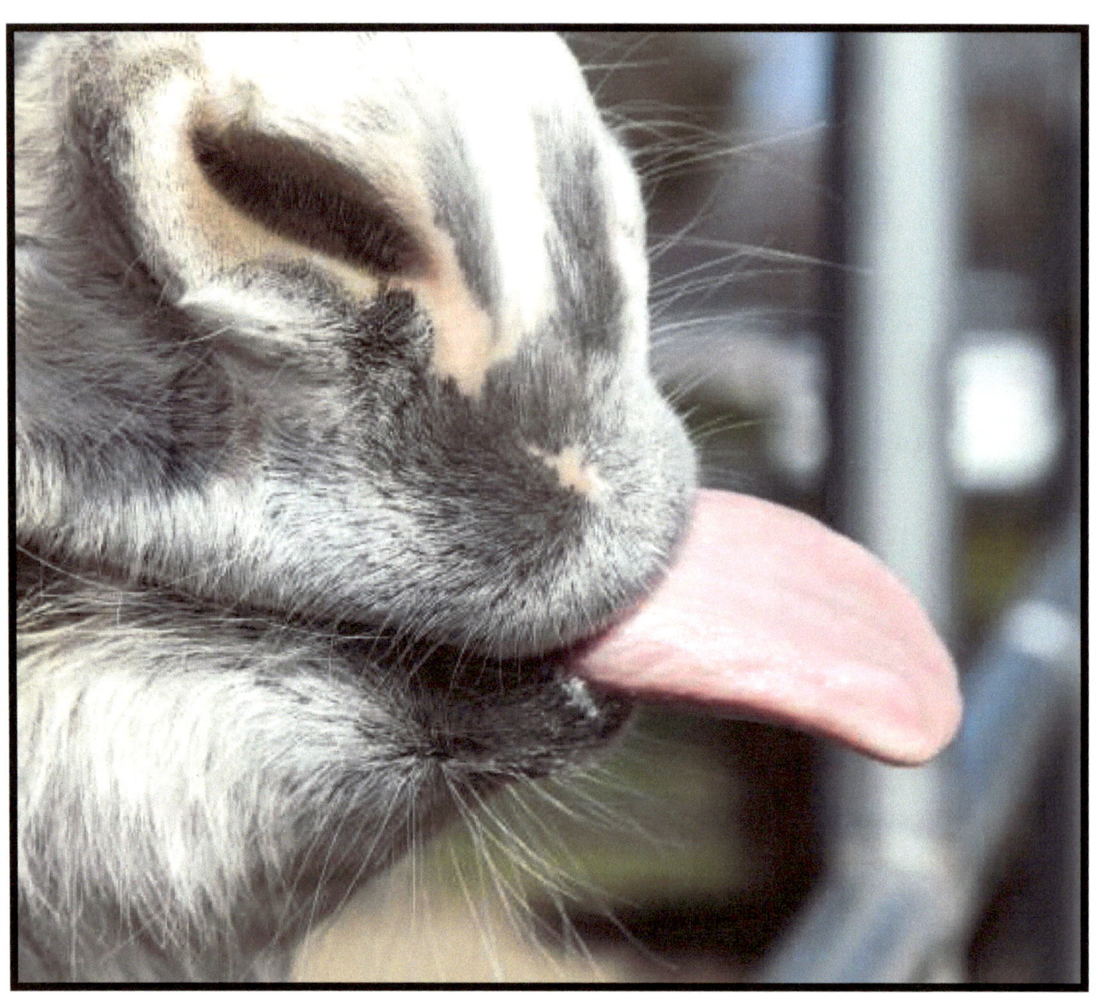

Andy is a spotted, boy donkey and he is very silly. He likes to stick out his tongue and make everyone laugh at his funny faces.

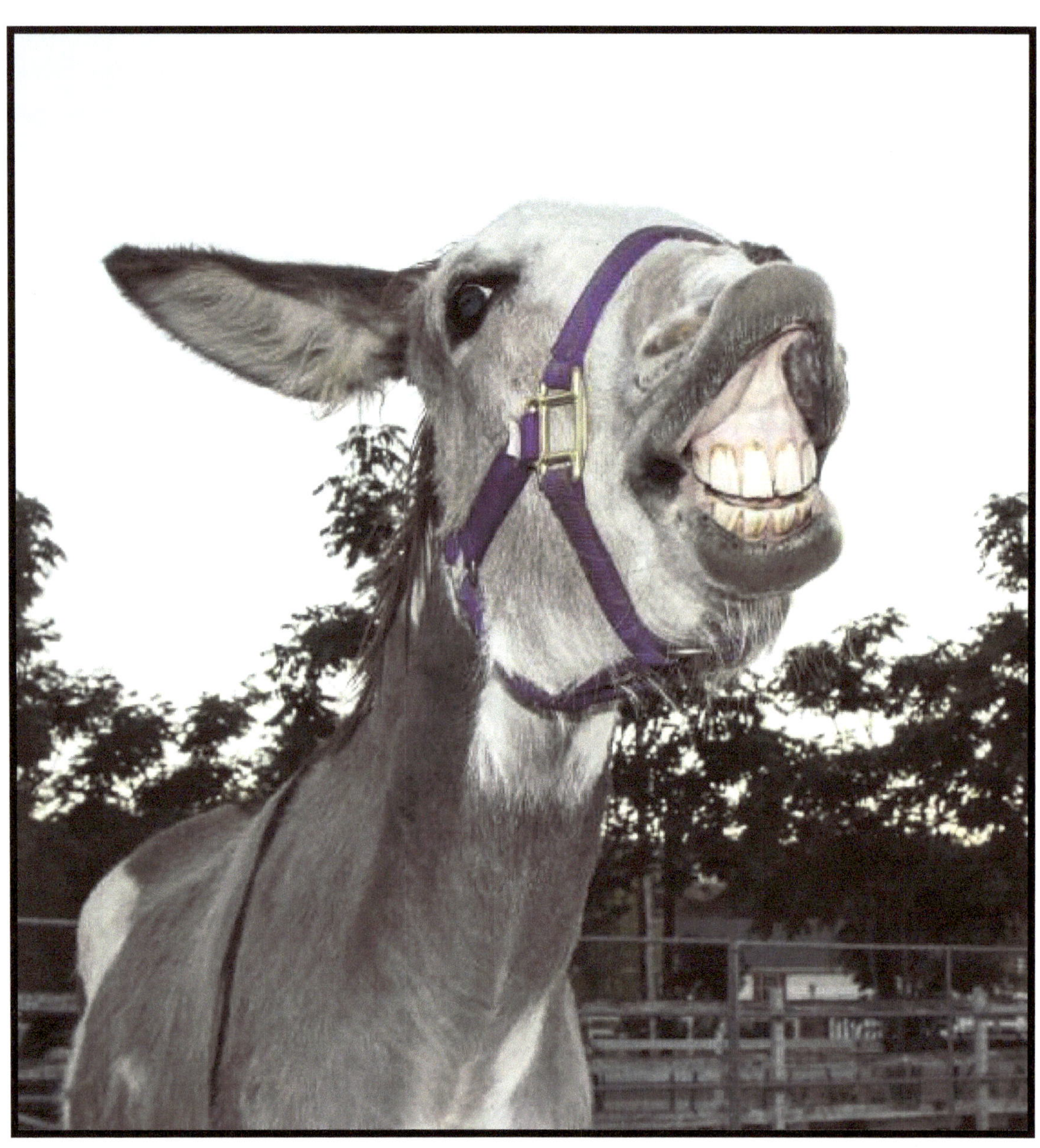

He loves to show his teeth and smile. When he does, he often gets a treat. He likes that a lot.

Peyton told him, "Andy, don't stick out your tongue, that's kind of rude, but it is kind of funny too."

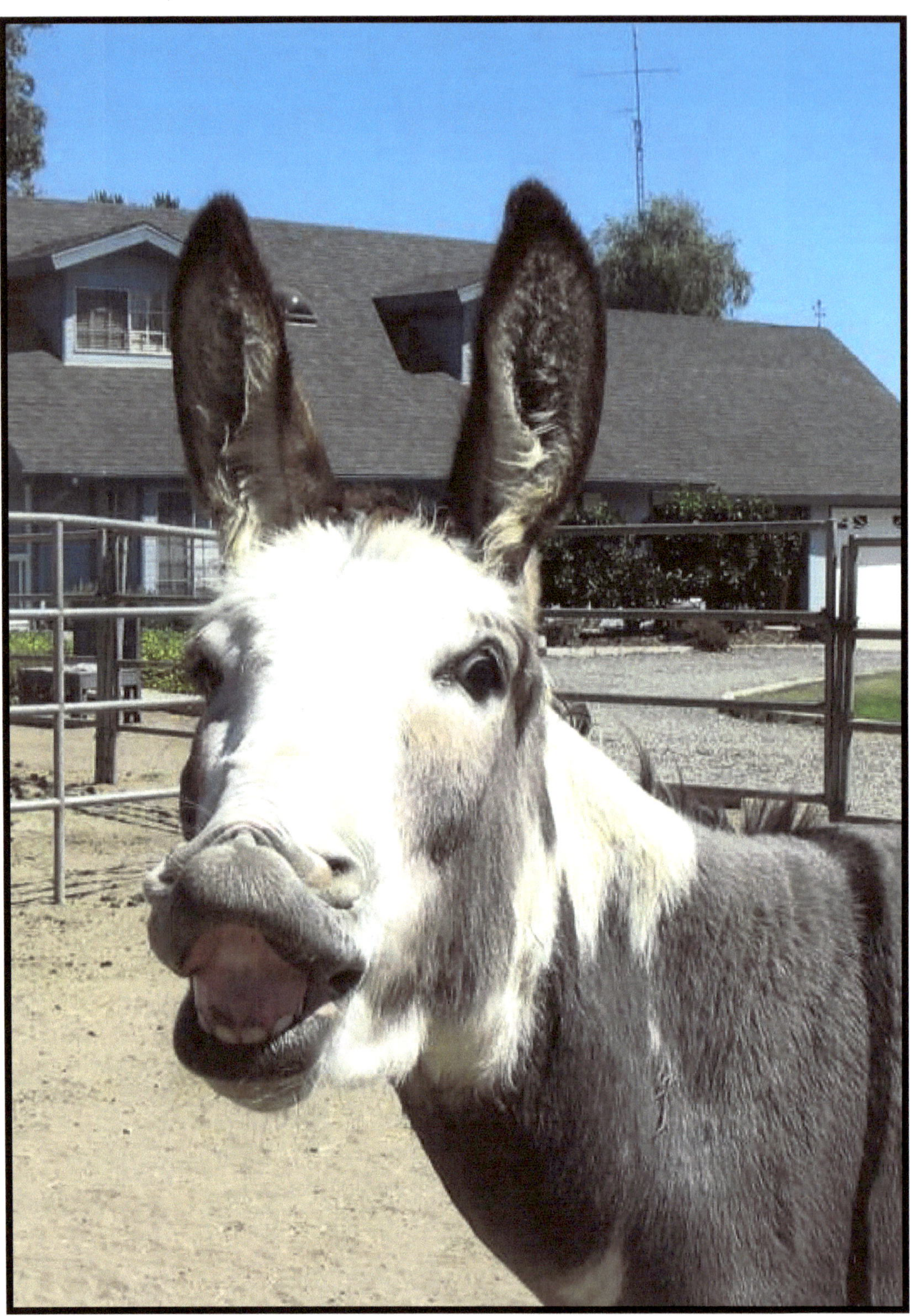

The children did not know that donkeys like to be so silly and that making funny faces, smiling and wearing hats is just part of a good day for a donkey.

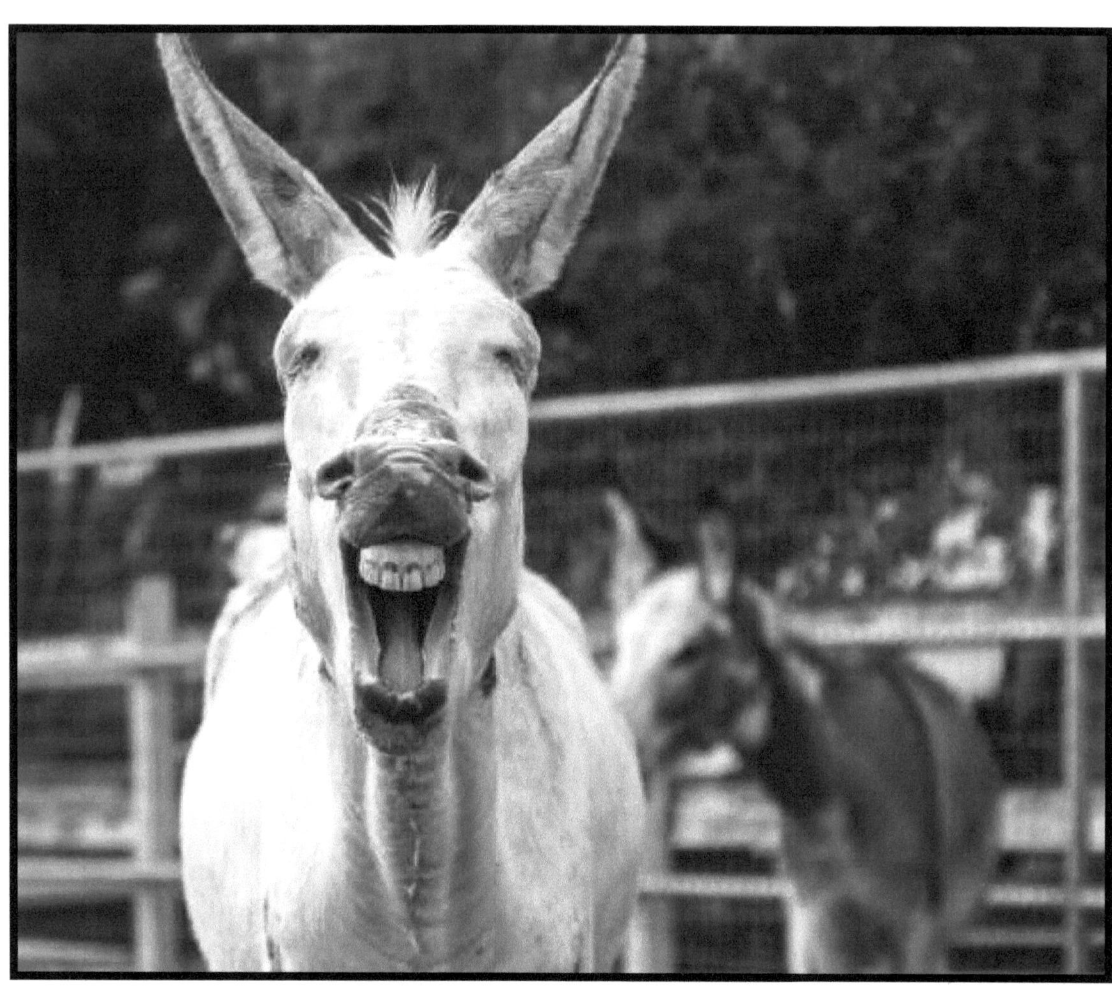

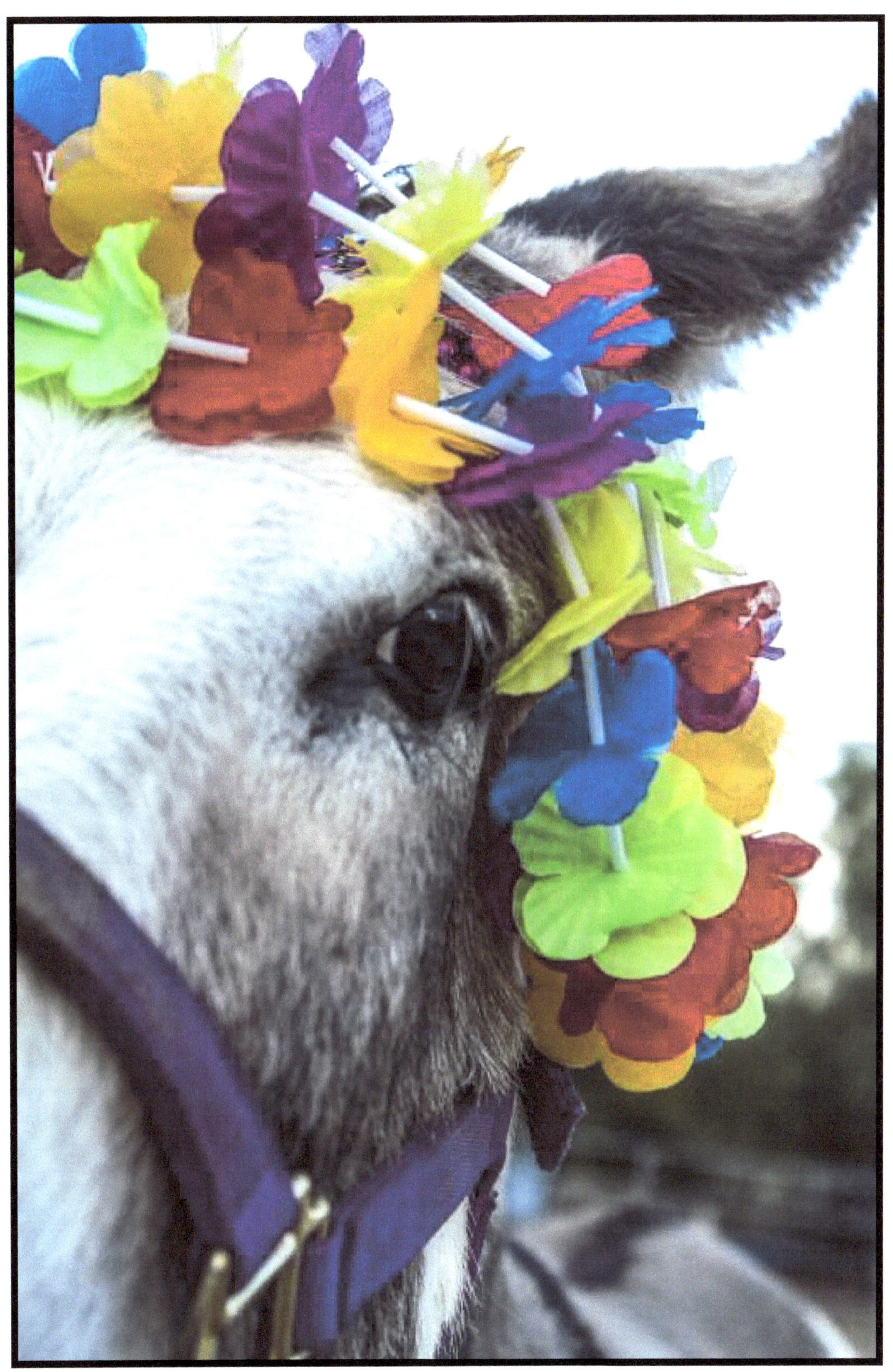

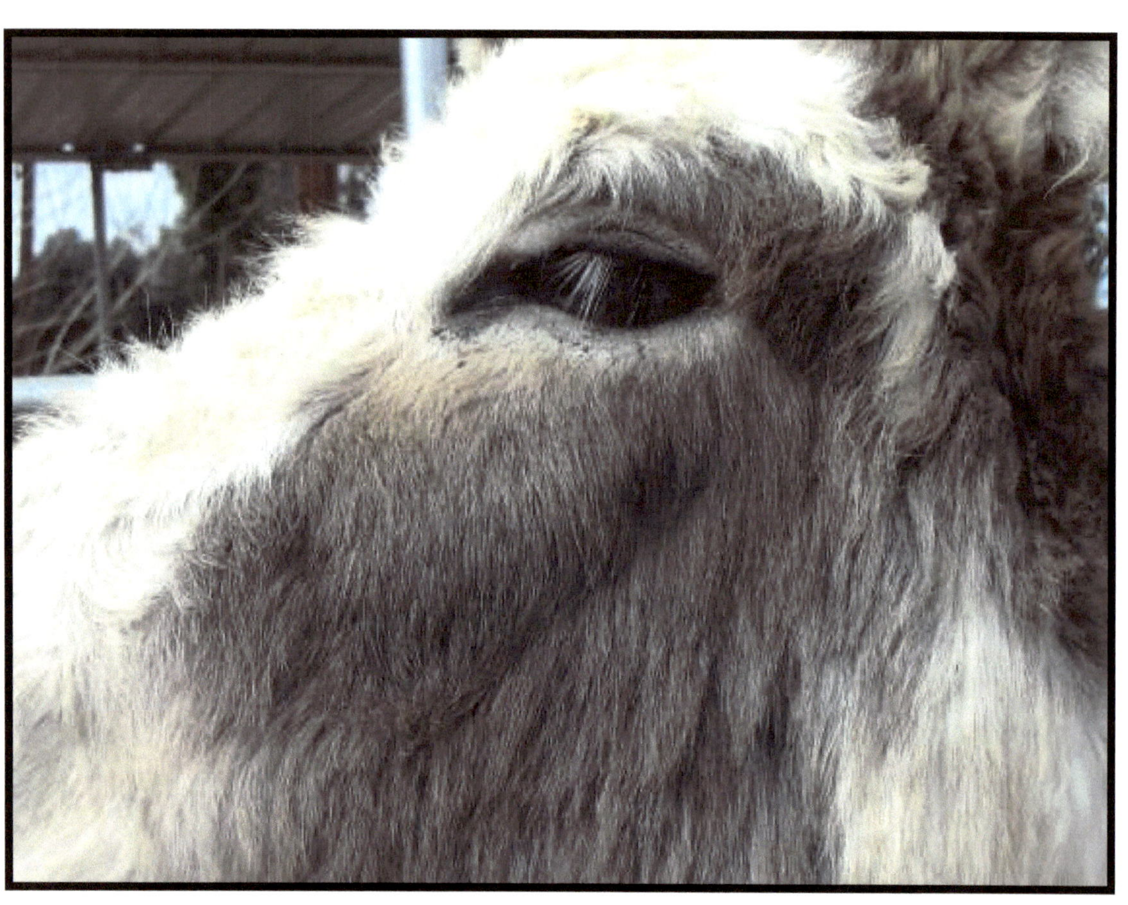

Donkeys have long eyelashes and kind gentle eyes.

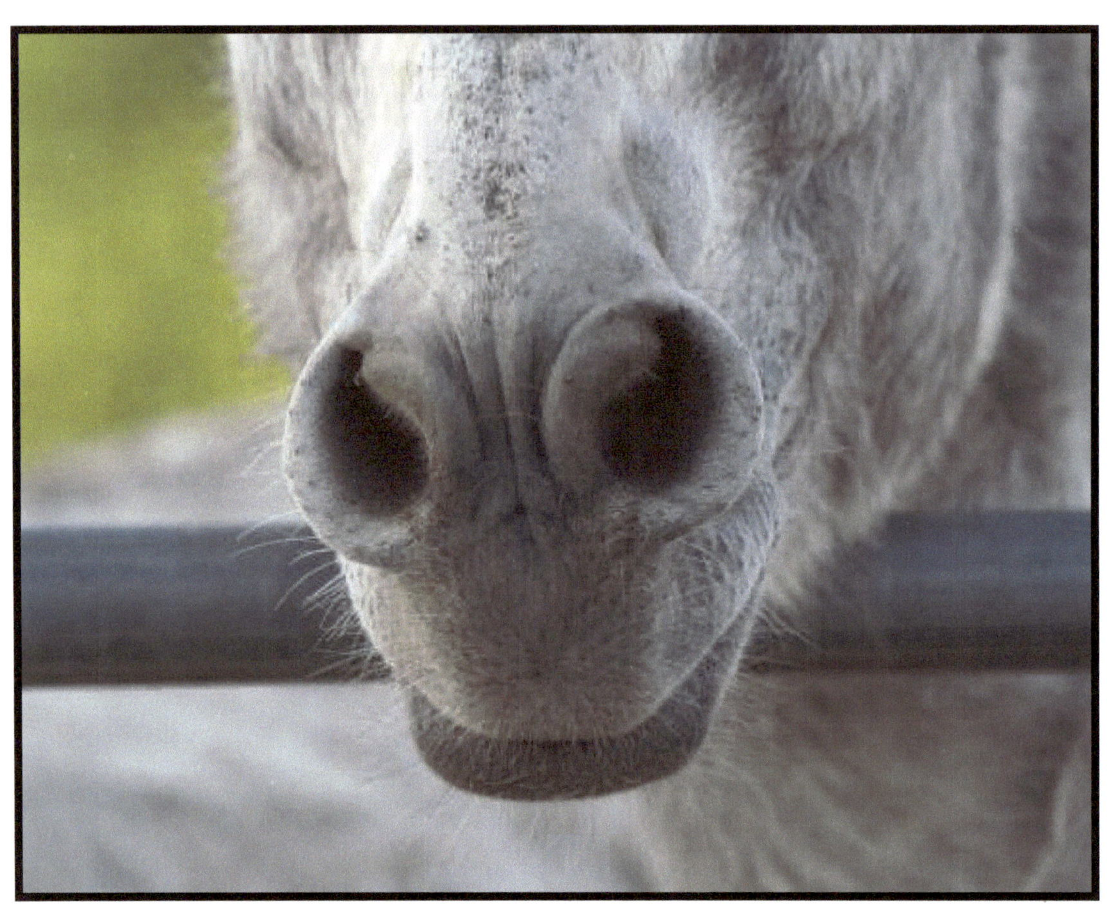

Donkey's noses are called muzzles;

they are very soft and kissable.

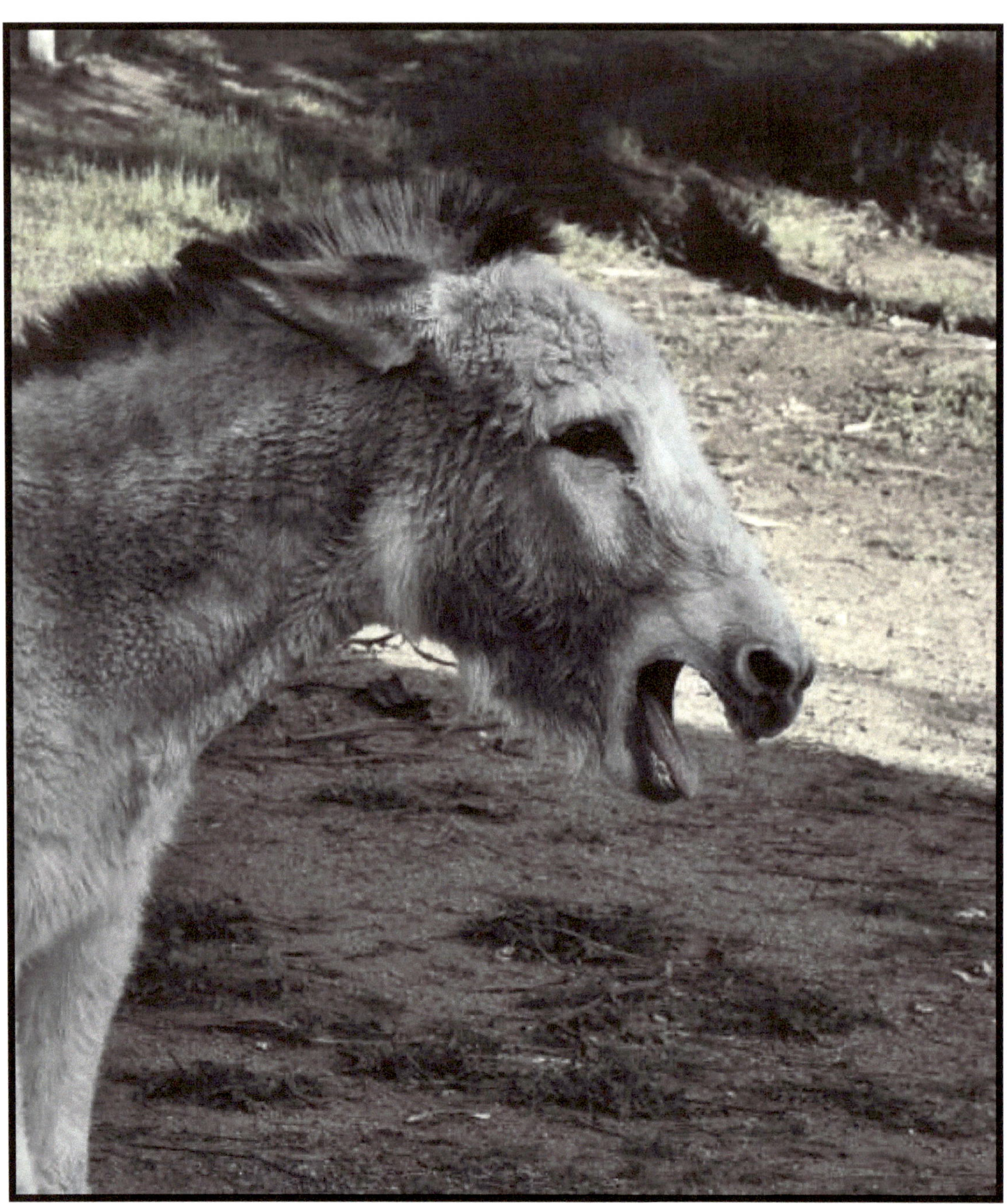

Donkeys like to talk to you, making a 'hee haw' noise. This is called braying. It sounds very loud and very funny.

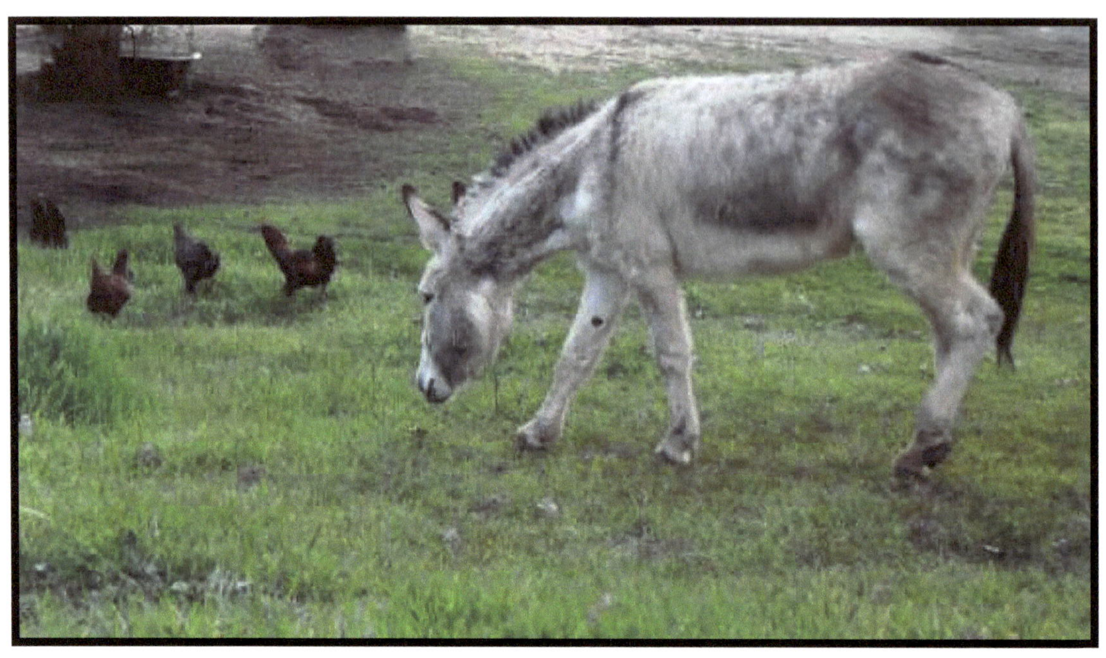

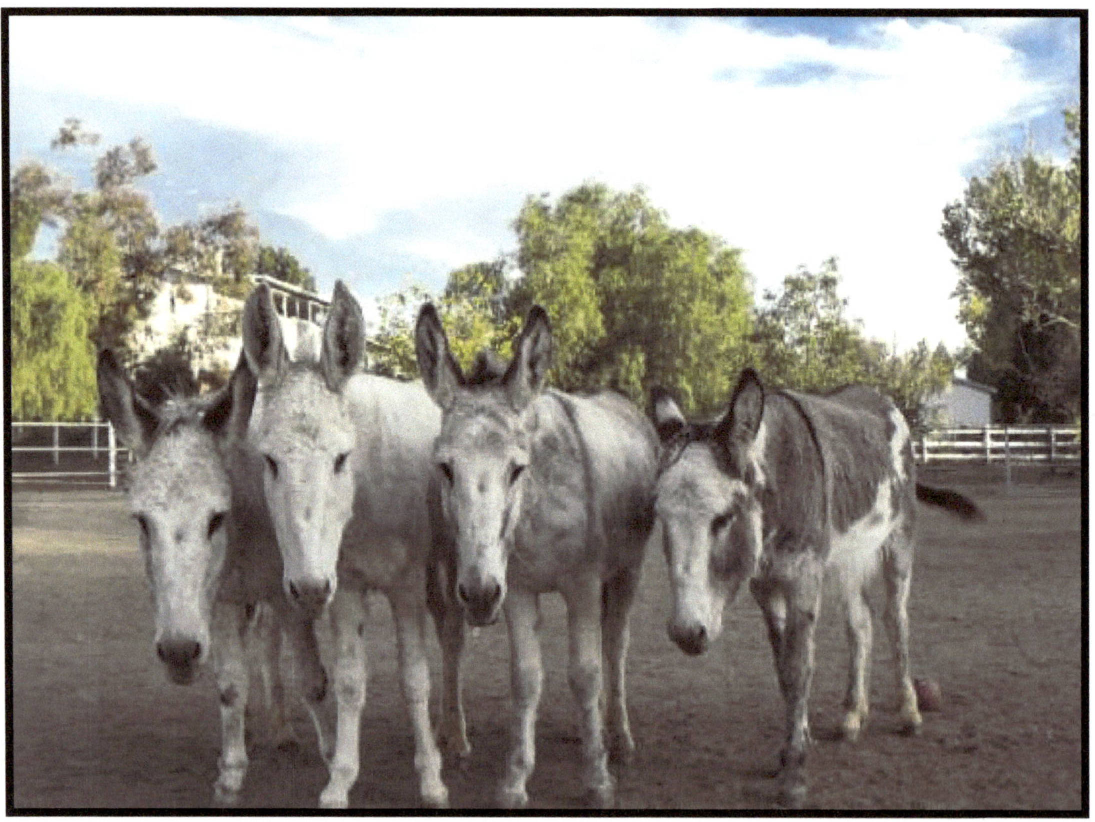

The donkeys like to play with the chickens at Grampa's ranch.

They run and play in the pasture together.

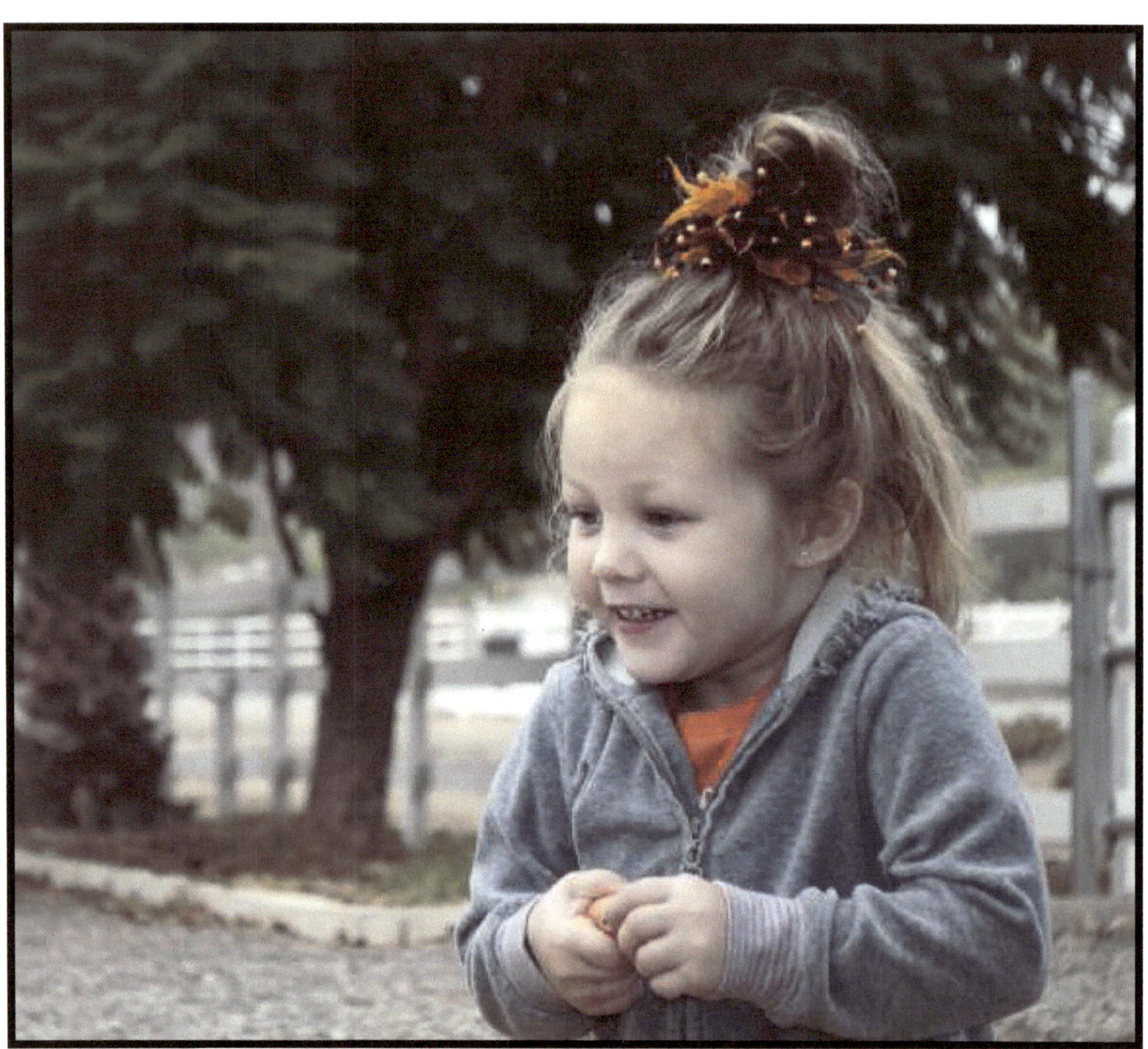

When Peyton was finished feeding the donkeys some treats, she asked, "Can I ride a donkey Gramma. Please?"

Gramma said, "Sure you can Peyton, but let's get Grampa and Mommy to help us."

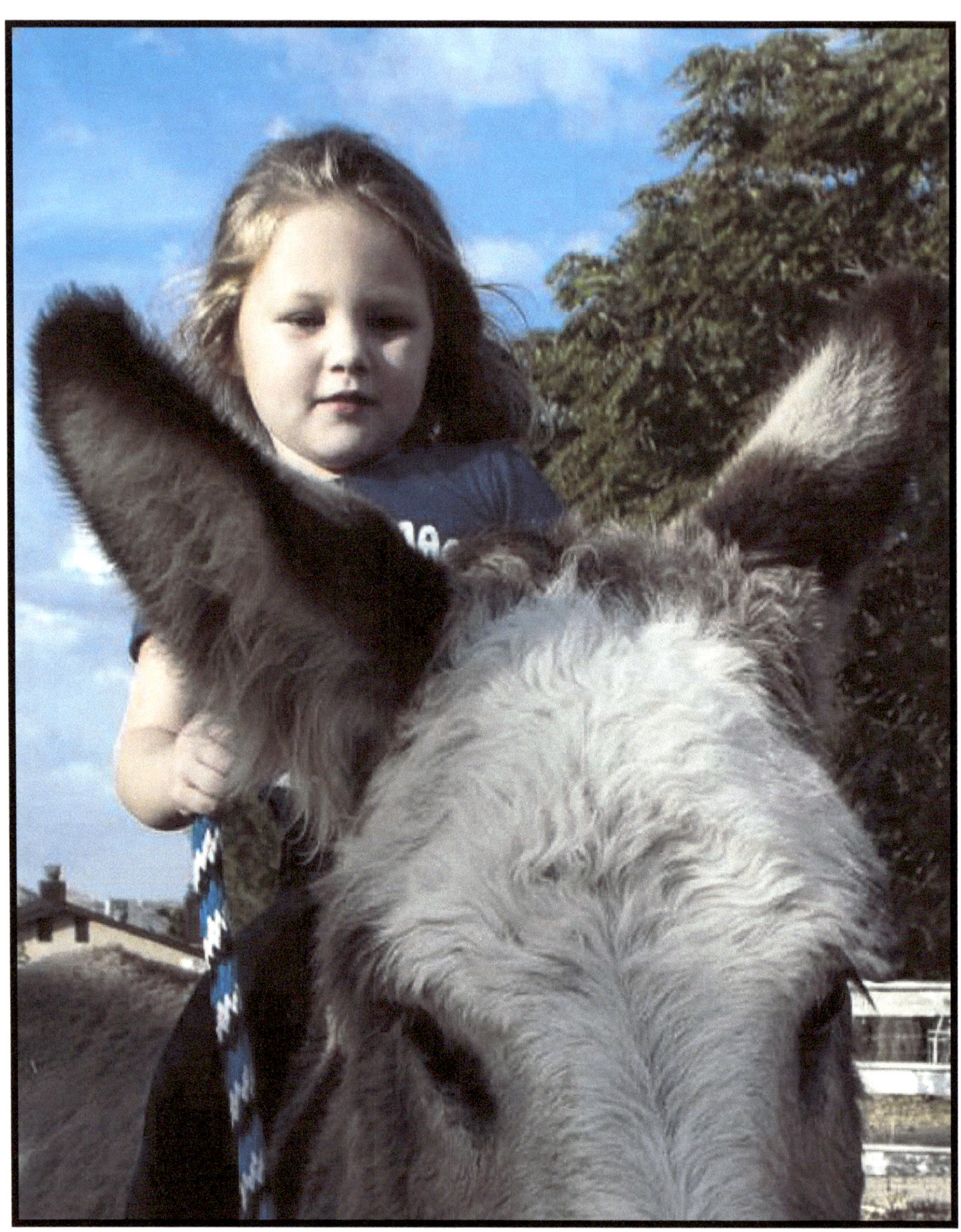

Grampa Dave came out to help. He lifted Peyton up onto Andy's back. She flashed him a huge smile.

Peyton was so excited to be on Andy's back.

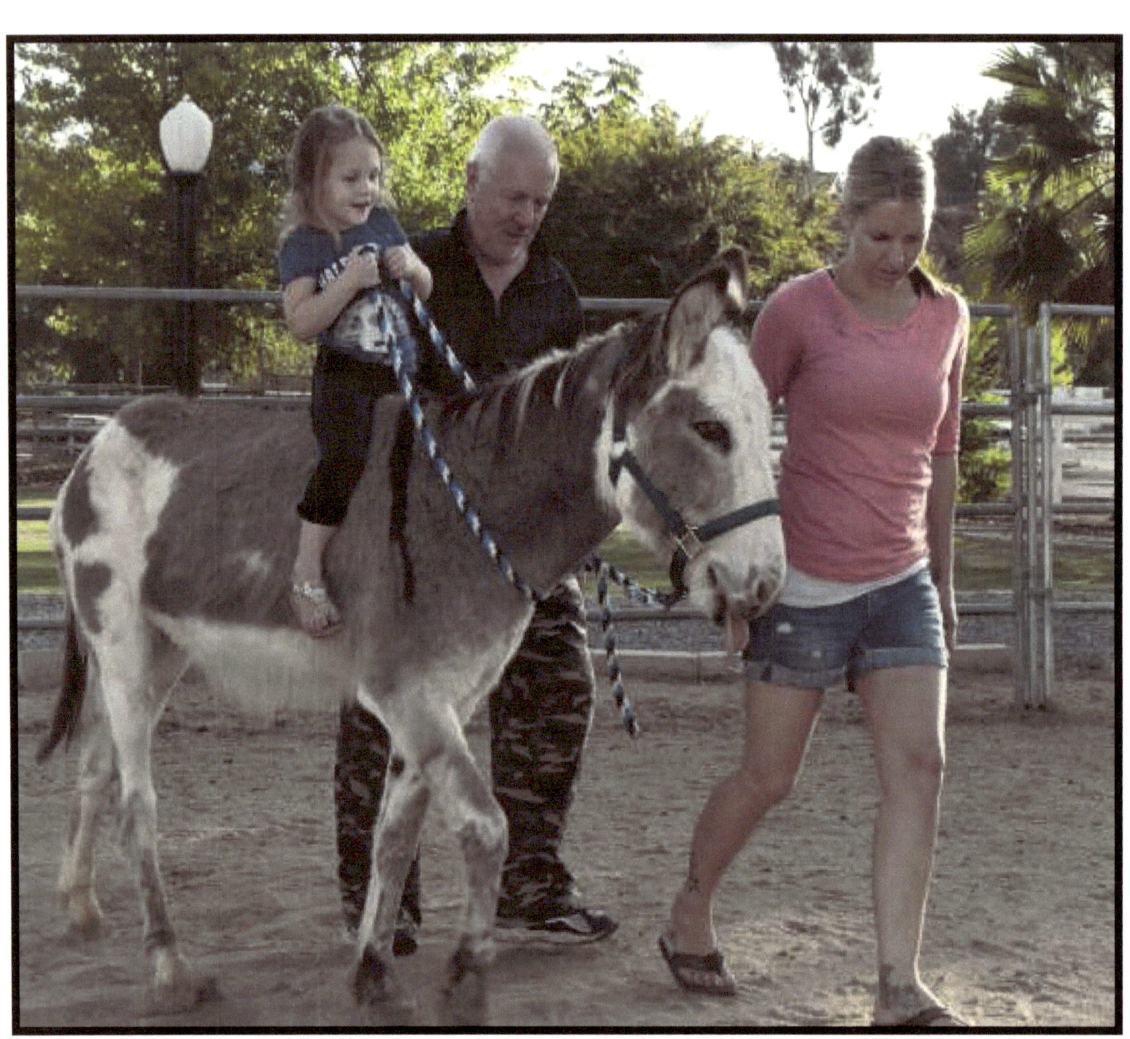

With the help of Grampa and Mommy, Peyton rode on Andy's back around and around and around the donkey pen. Here is Andy, with his tongue sticking out, and Peyton with a big happy smile.

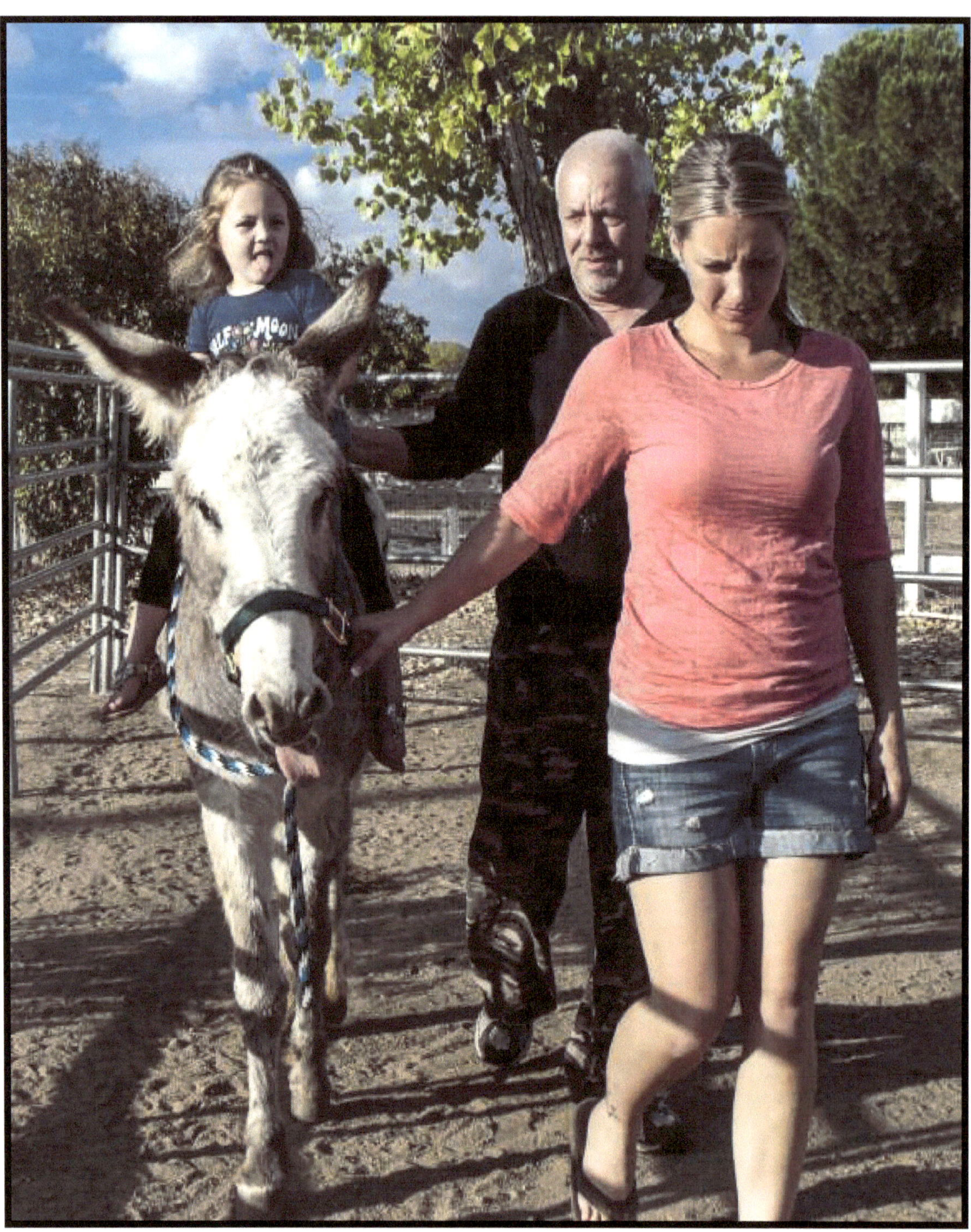

Peyton joined in with Andy and stuck out her tongue too.

What fun it was to ride a donkey!

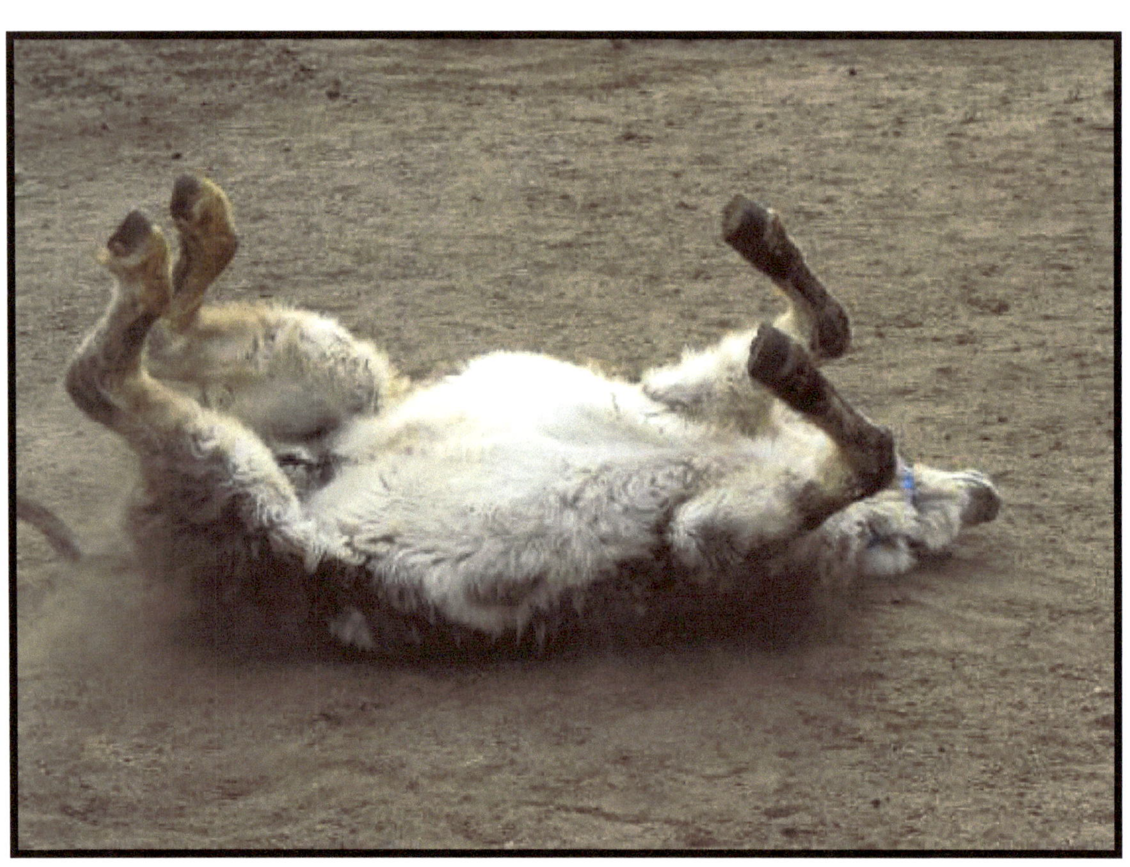

This was a good day for everyone! After the ride was over, Andy plopped down on the ground and rolled and rolled and rolled, making us all laugh until our bellies hurt. "Donkeys are cute and silly." said Peyton.

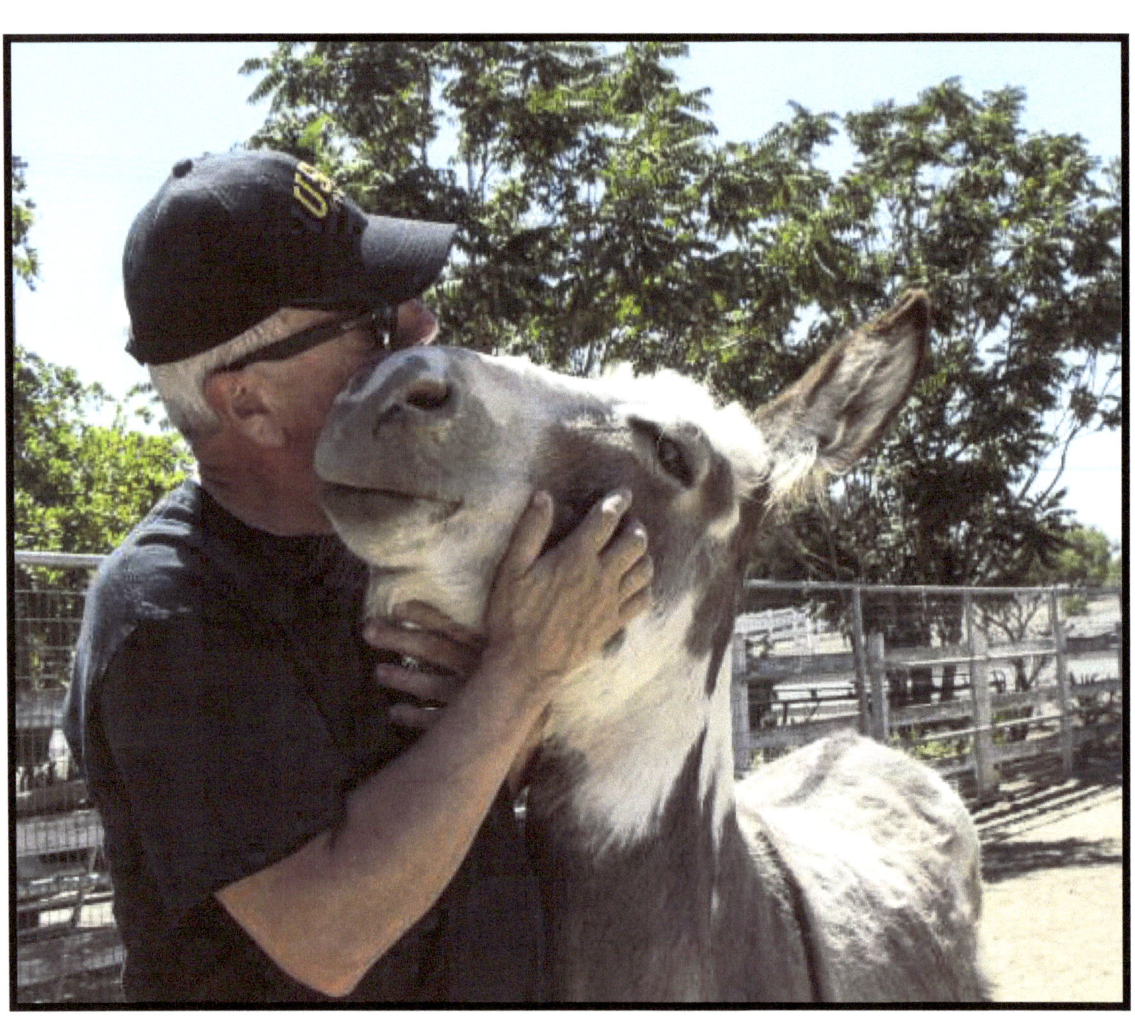

Grampa Dave gave Andy a big hug
for making us all laugh and smile.

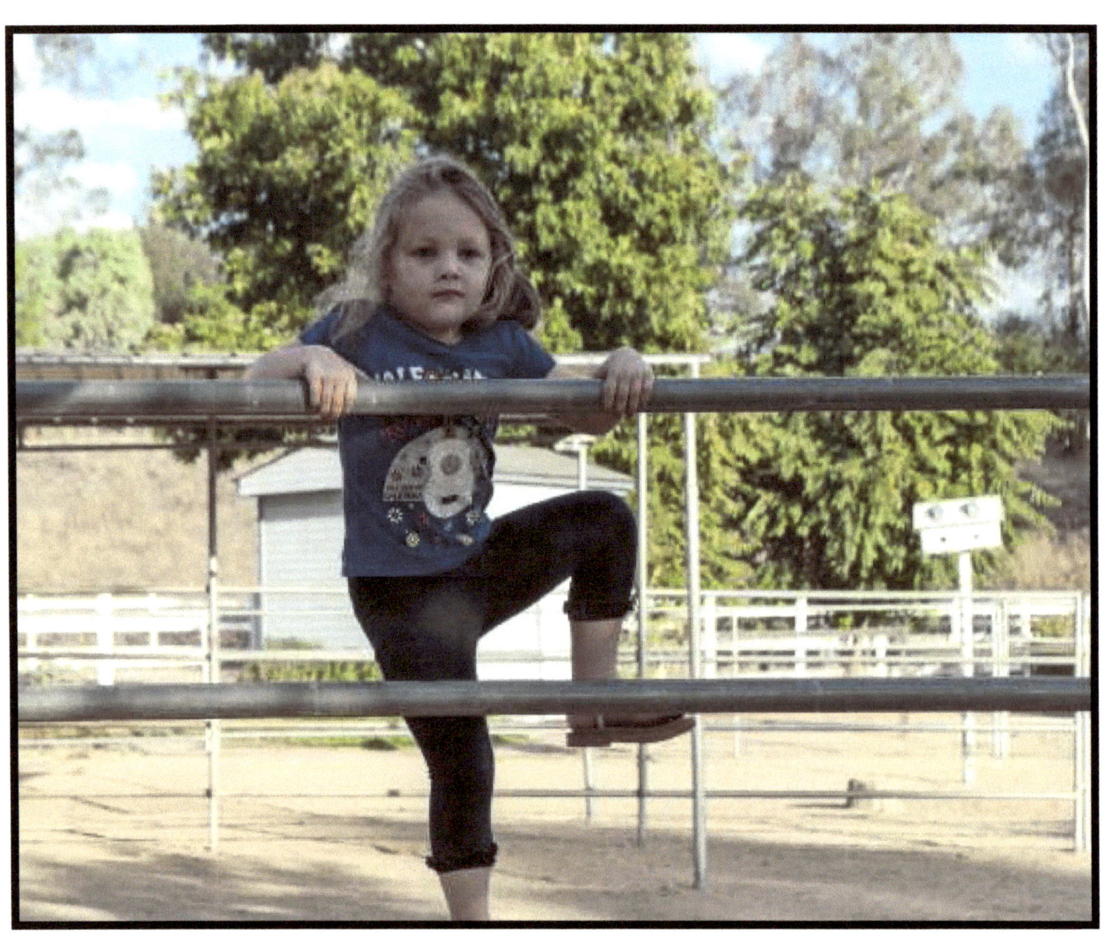

"Thank you for the ride Andy, I love you. I'll be back tomorrow with more treats."

THE END

Credits and Acknowledgements

To my family and friends who helped me pursue my dream of writing a children's book, I thank you from the bottom of my heart. A very special thank you to my husband, David, and my daughter Jennifer, her husband Loren and my adorable grandkids, Peyton and Hunter who helped inspire me to write this book.

I love you all, to the moon and back!

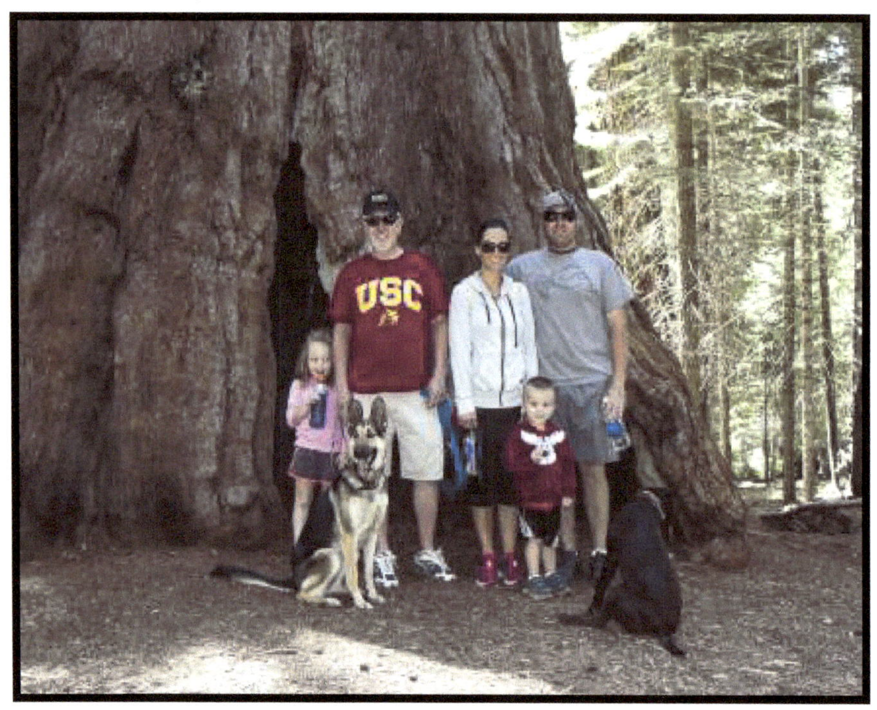

www.janiceCarabinePhotography.com

www.facebook.com/JaniceCarabinePhotography

Contact the Author -Carabinej@gmail.com

Visit the Donkeys at www.facebook.com/groups/46948171685

www.ingramcontent.com/pod-product-compliance
Lightning Source LLC
LaVergne TN
LVHW070152110826
845147LV00002B/383
9780615860183